HOME SWEET HOME

COLORING BOOK

HOME SWEET HOME
COLORING BOOK

SIRIUS

SIRIUS

This edition published in 2022 by Sirius Publishing, a division of
Arcturus Publishing Limited,
26/27 Bickels Yard, 151–153 Bermondsey Street,
London SE1 3HA

ISBN: 978-1-3988-1472-1
CH010157NT

Printed in China

INTRODUCTION

Whether it's the place you come back to after a long day at work, the promise of familiarity after a long vacation, or the family house where you grew up—and where you return to, home means different things to all of us at different times. The images in this coloring book have been selected to give a picture of all aspects of home. They encompass cozy living rooms, peaceful bedrooms you can retire to at night, and bustling kitchens where you can just imagine cooking and baking going on. There are also other aspects of home including gardens and garden equipment, a book nook you can retreat to and read, as well as cupboards and cabinets packed with all the necessities of home.

Coloring in is a great way to relax and unwind, allowing you to concentrate on creativity while shutting out the cares of the day. Take a selection of colored pencils, choose a comfortable spot to sit, and start to color your own artistic vision.

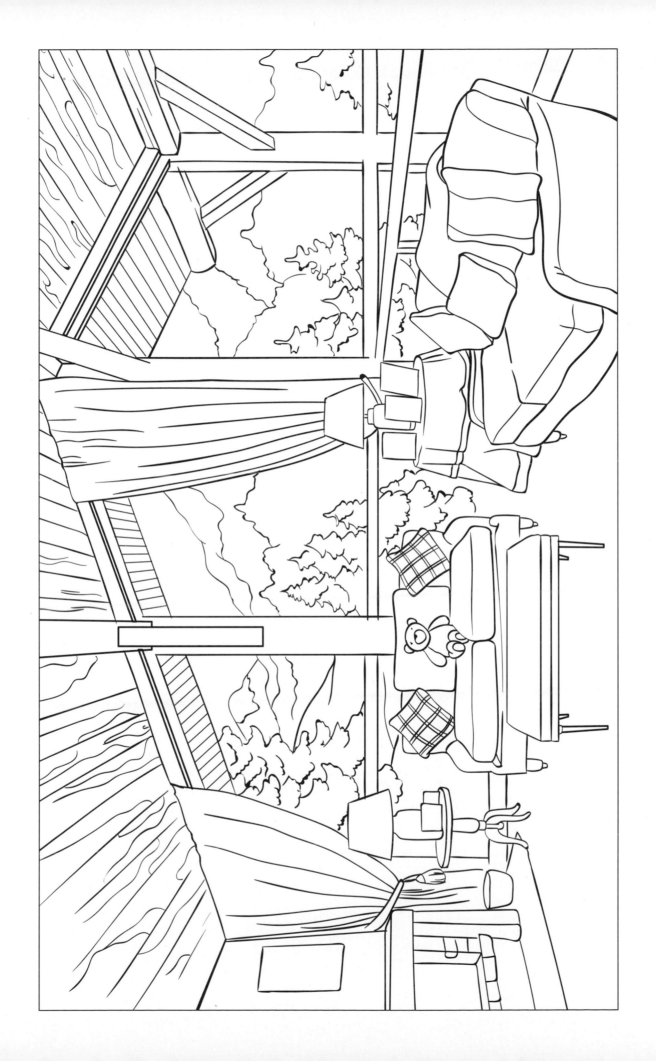

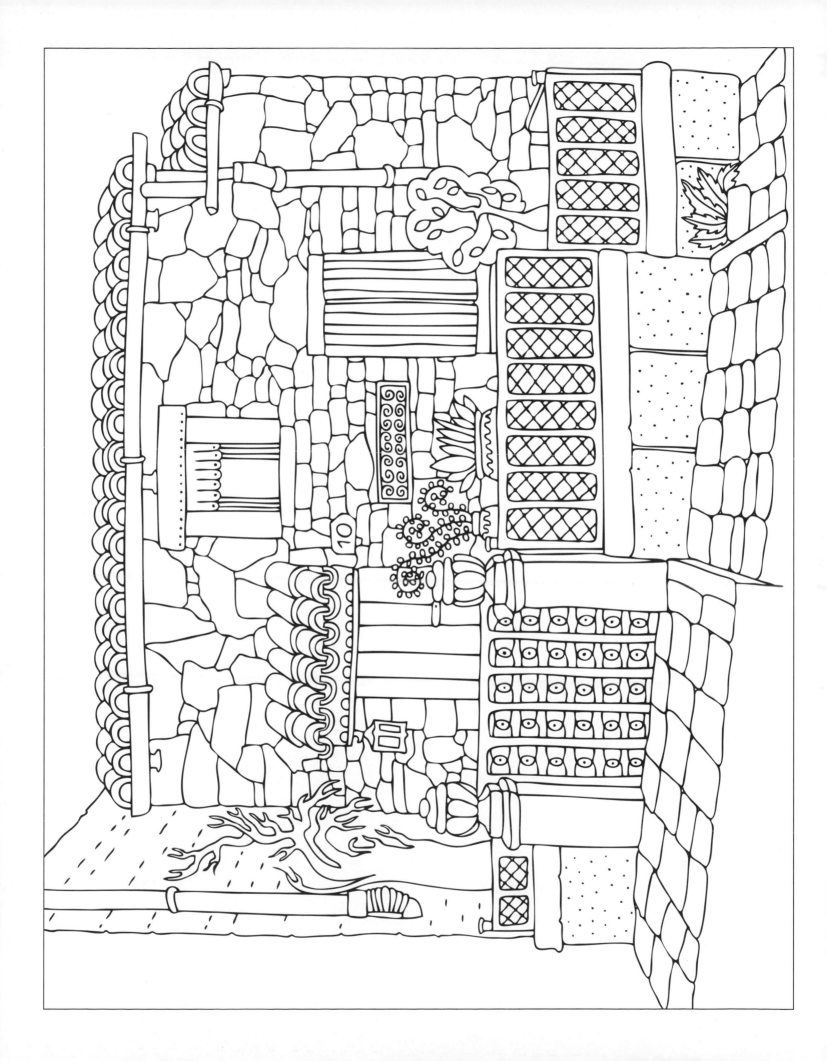

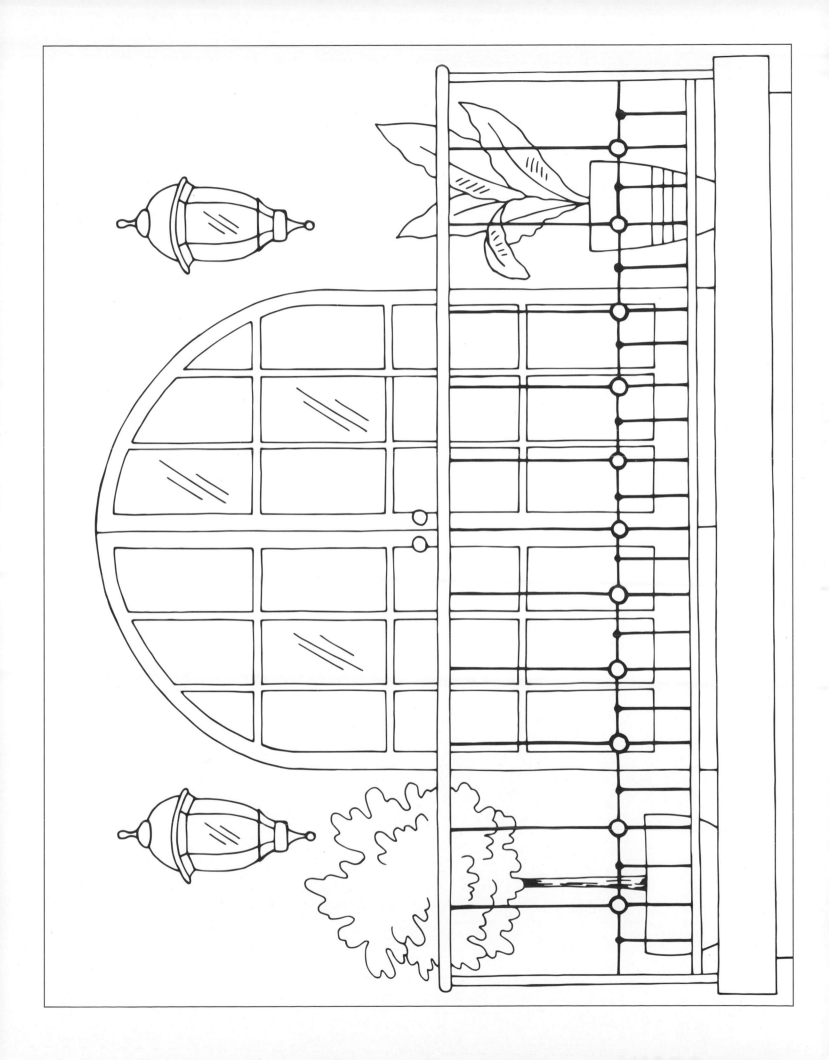

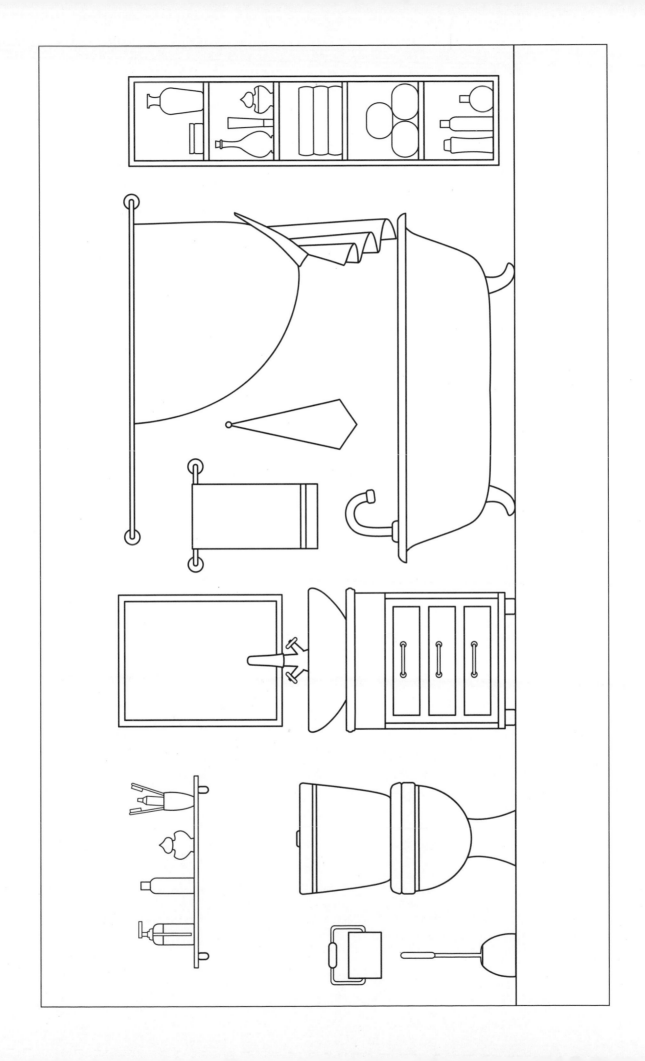

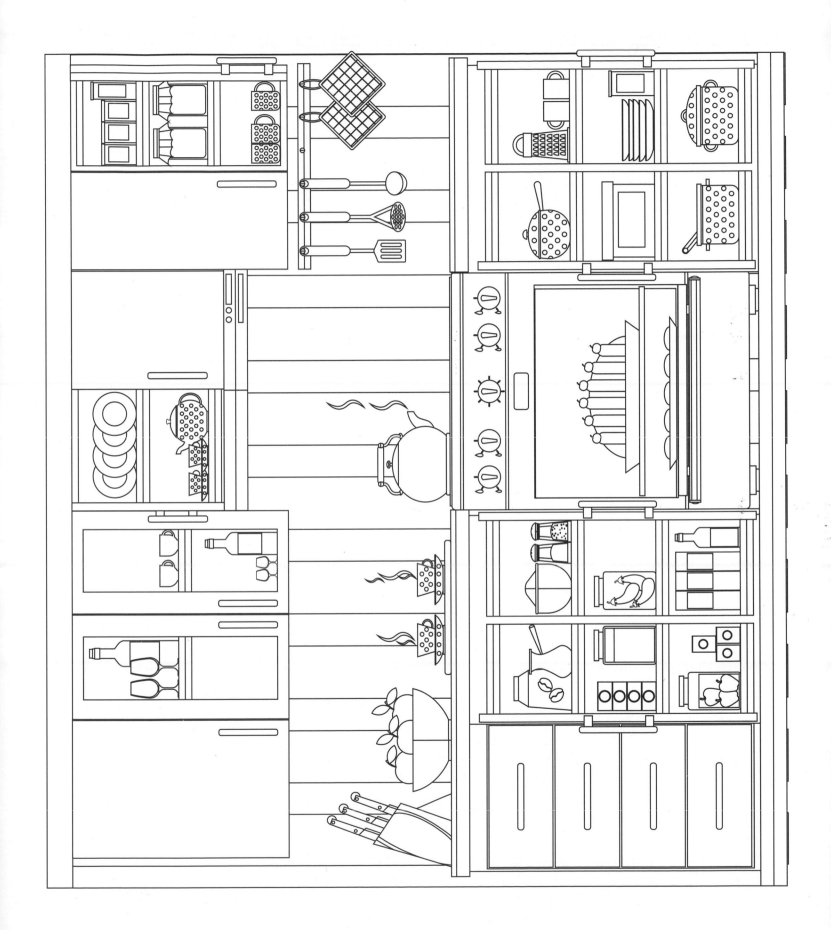

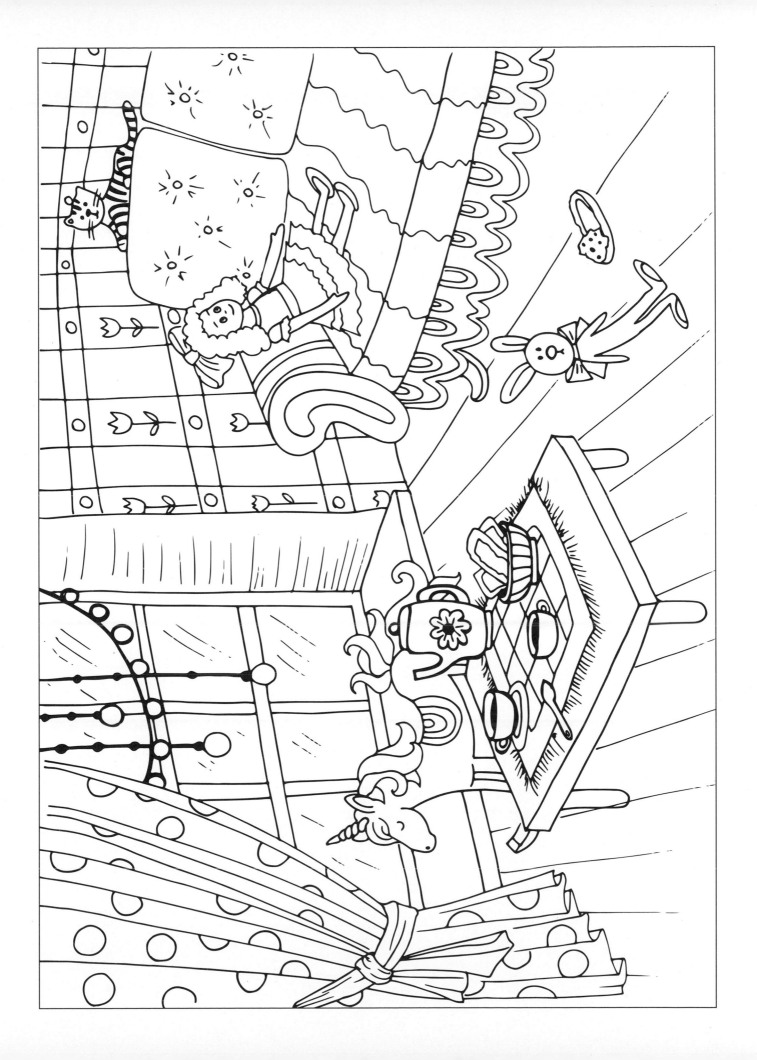

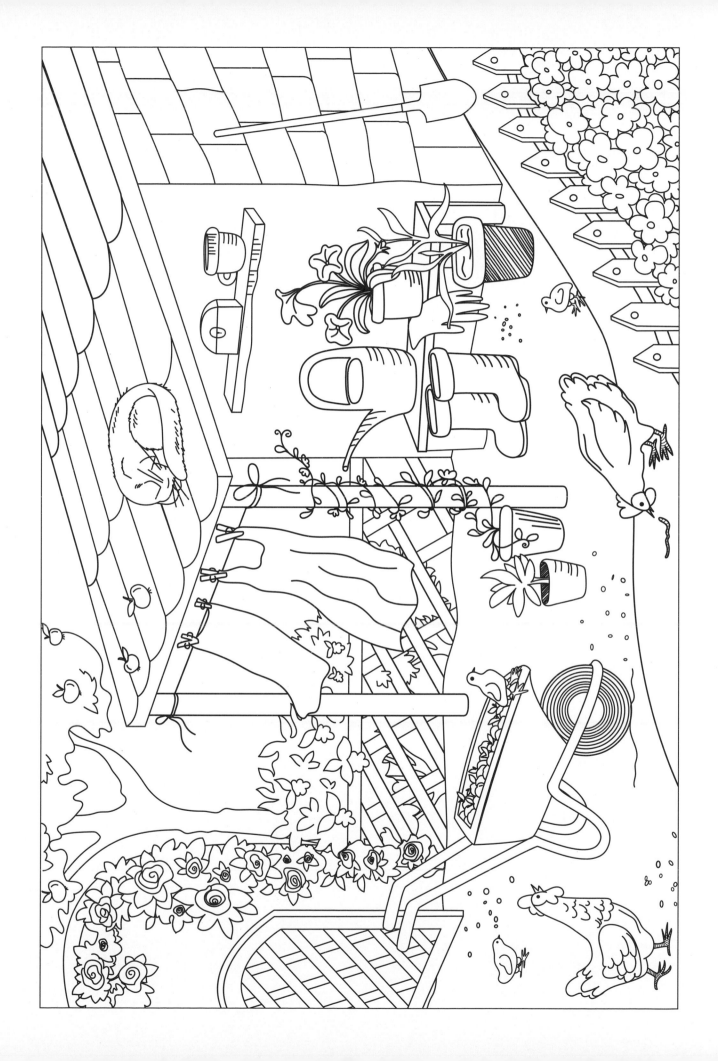

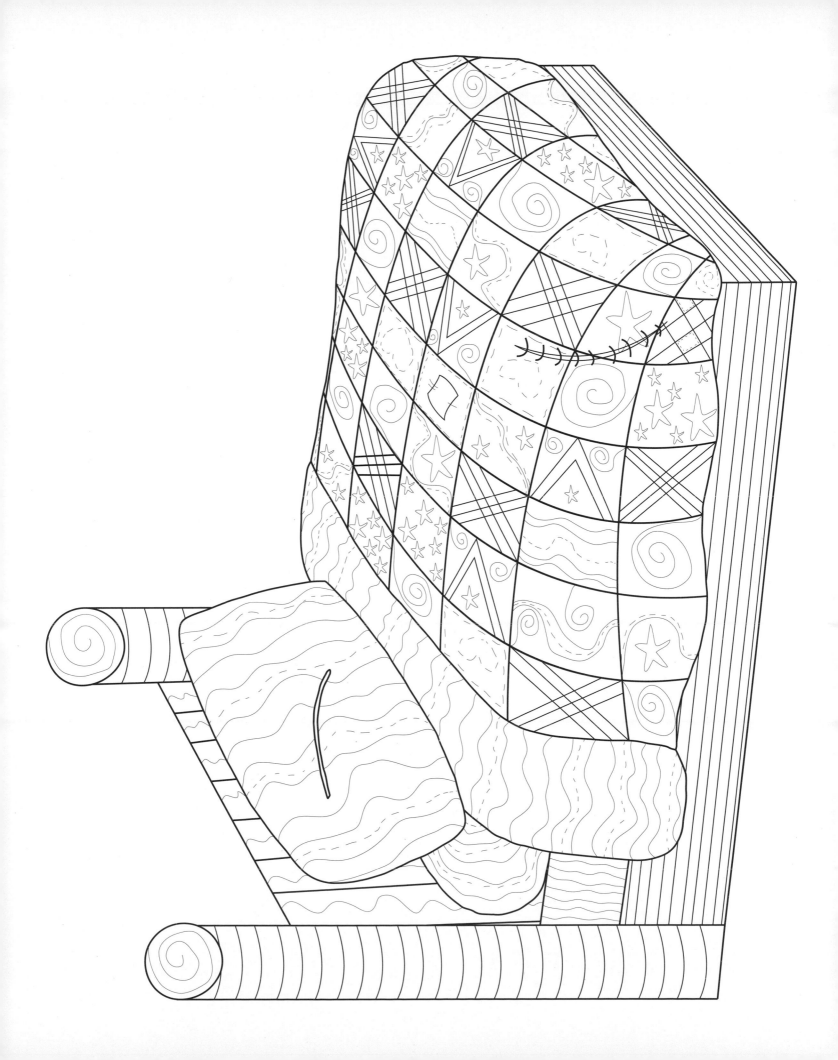

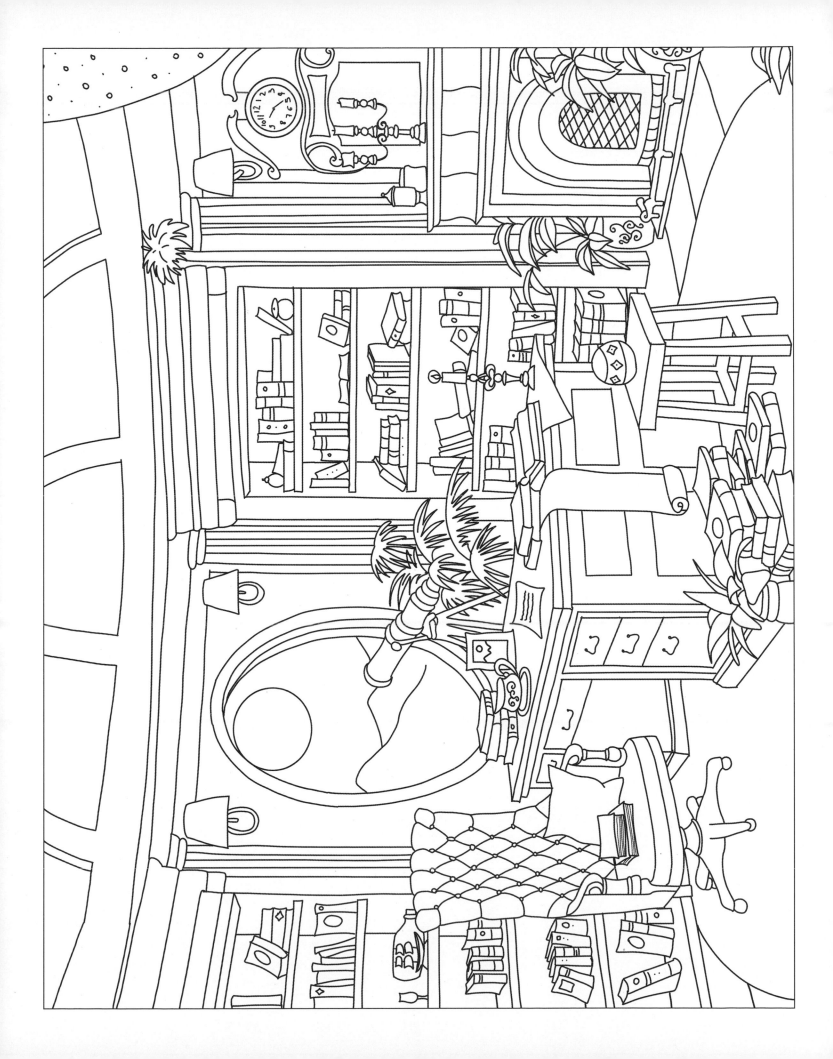

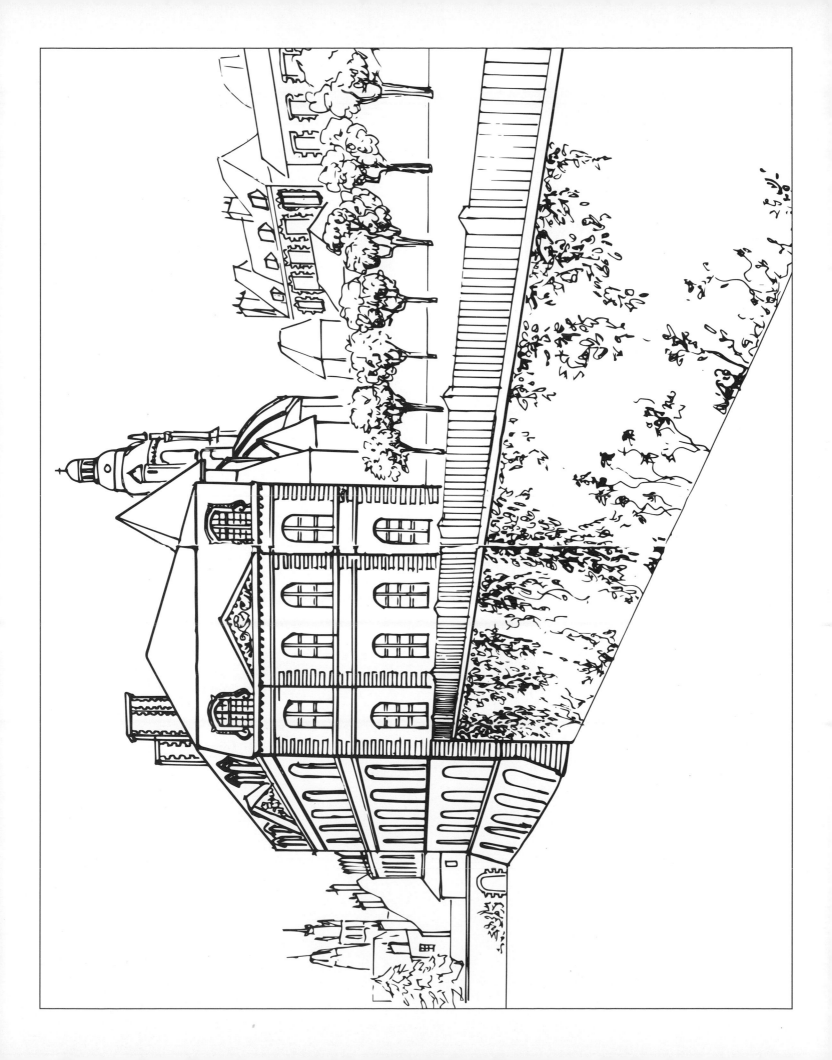

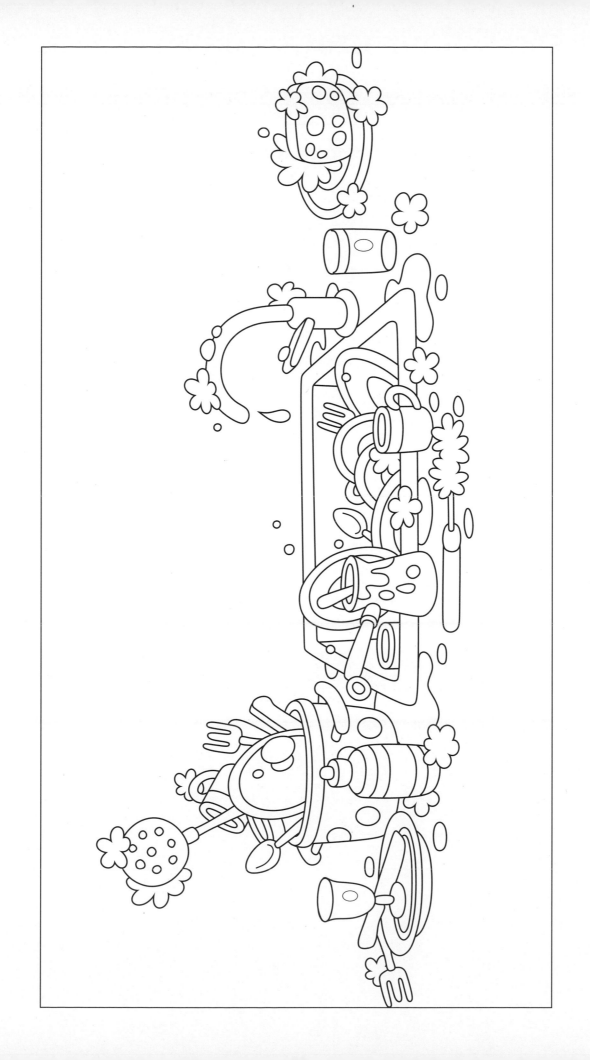

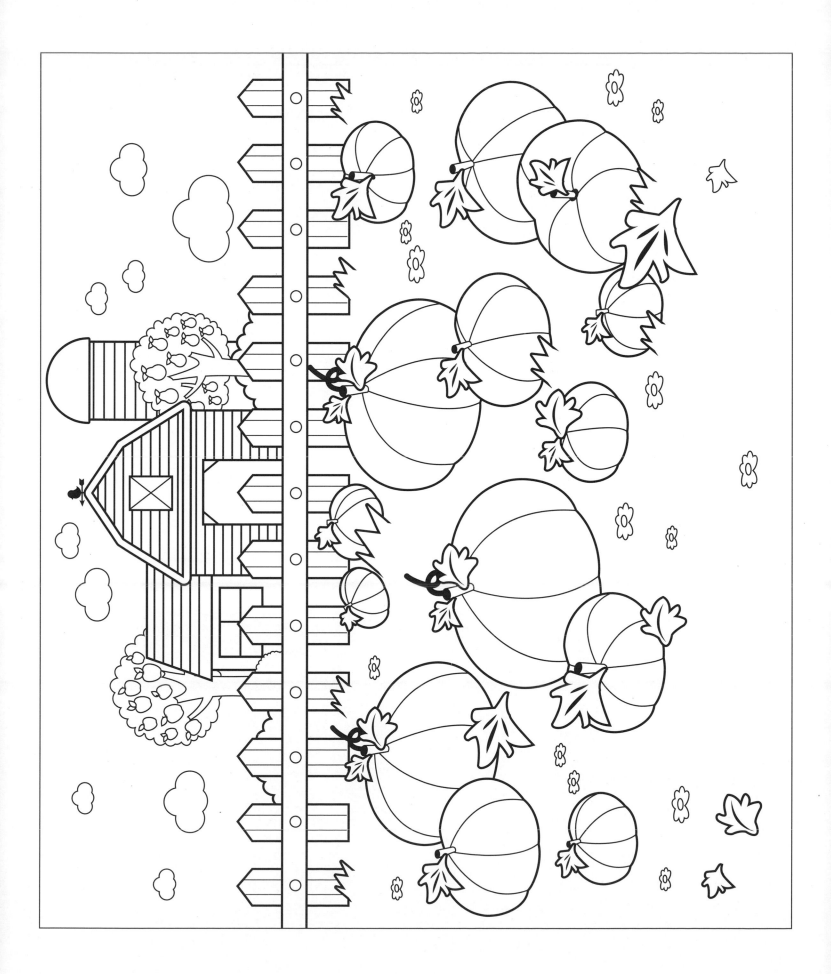

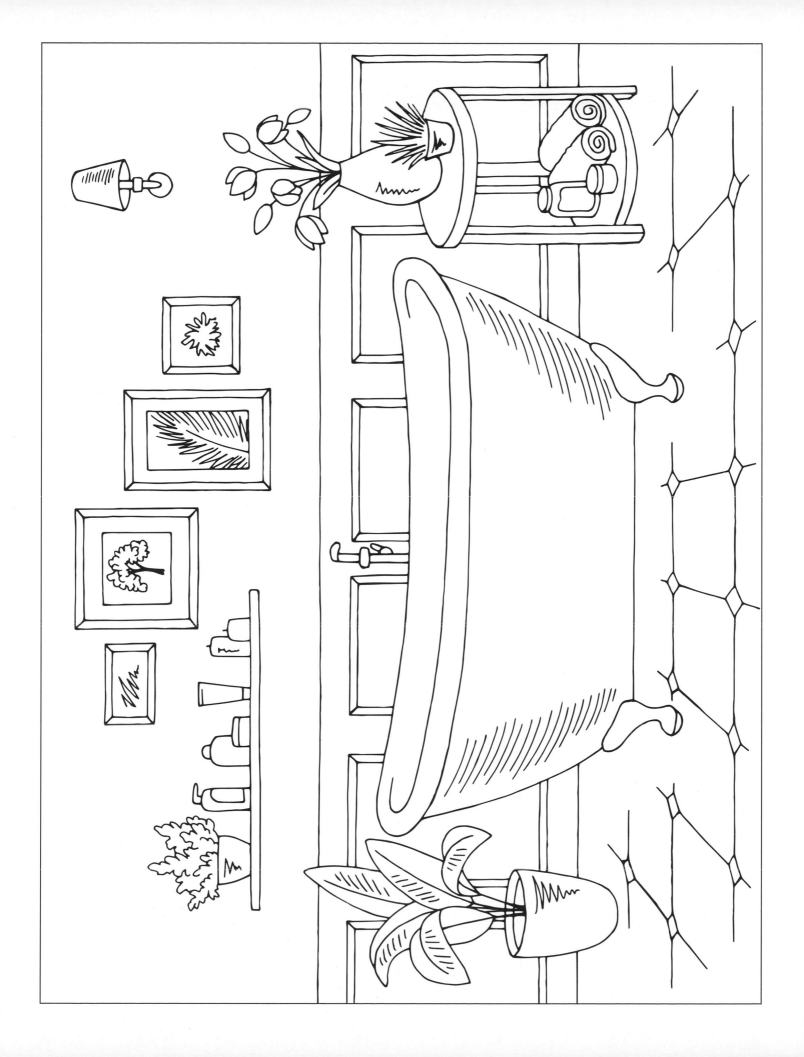

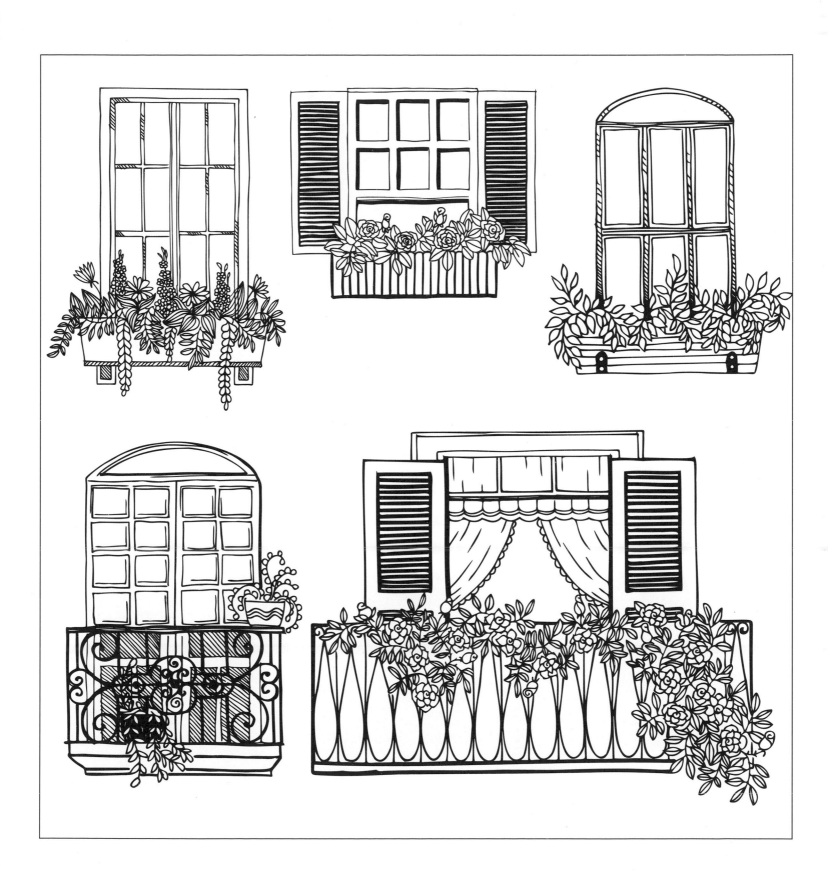

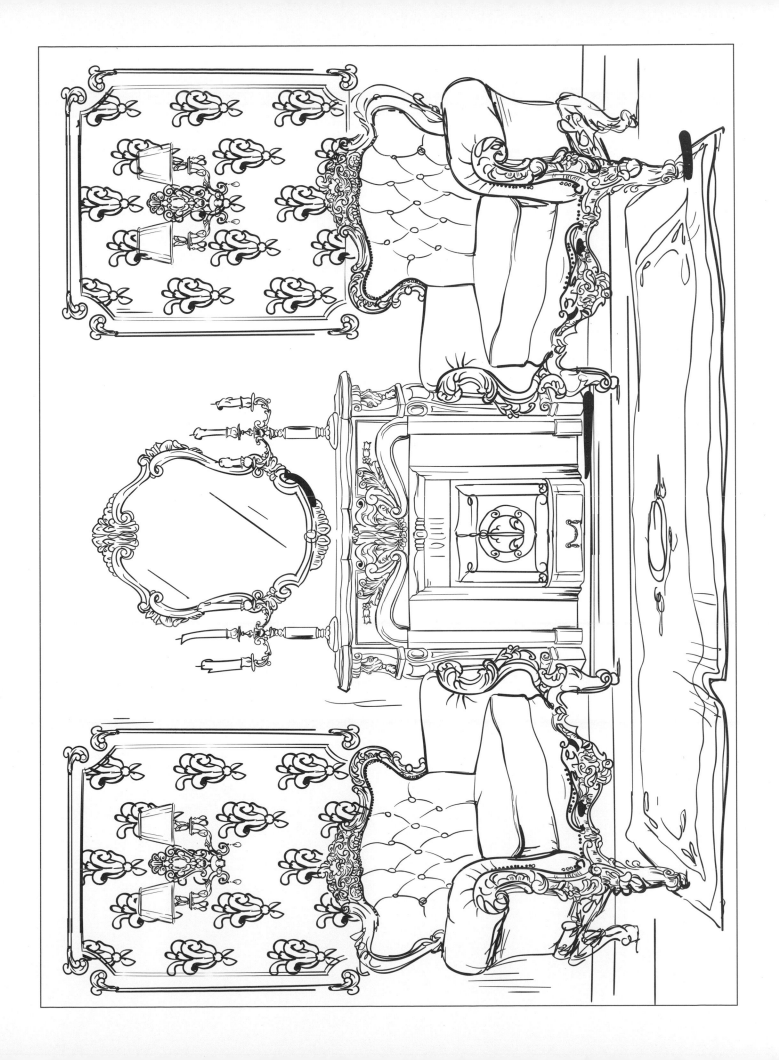

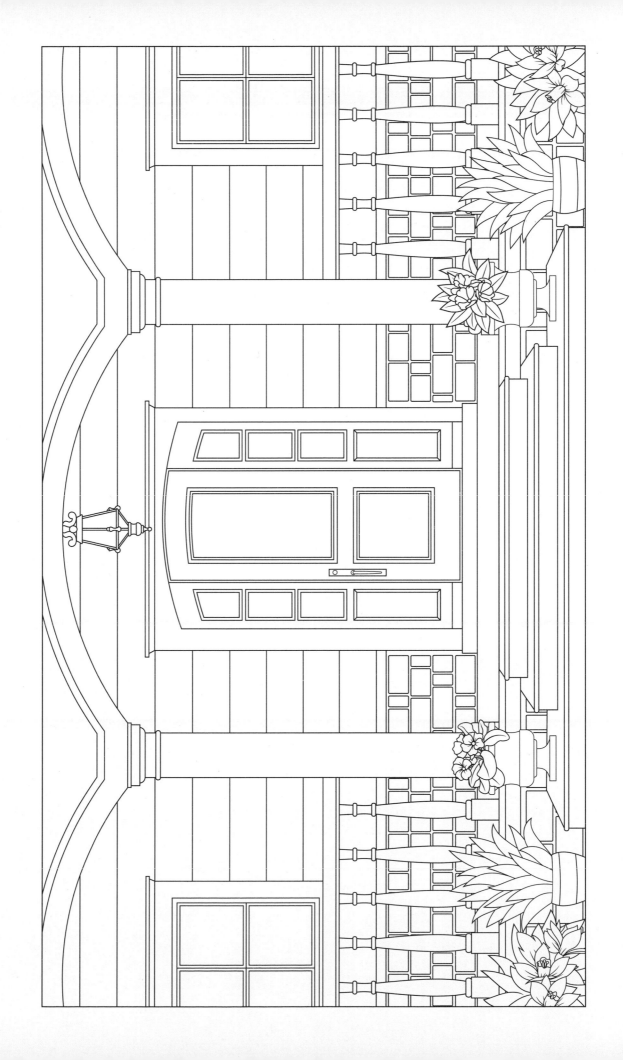